COMPARING
ANIMAL TRAITS

OSTRICHES

FAST FLIGHTLESS BIRDS

LAURA HAMILTON WAXMAN

Lerner Publications ◆ Minneapolis

For Bernard, a wonderful dad and granddad

Lerner Publications Company
A division of Lerner Publishing Group, Inc.
241 First Avenue North
Minneapolis, MN 55401 USA

For reading levels and more information, look up this title at www.lernerbooks.com.

Photo Acknowledgments

The images in this book are used with the permission of: © Sergei25/Shutterstock.com, p. 1; © Robert Henno/Alamy, p. 4; © Amy N. Harris/Bigstock.com, p. 5; © travelbild.com/Alamy, p. 6; © Frans Lanting/ Mint Images/Getty Images, p. 7 (top); © Stefano Gambassi/Flickr Open/Getty Images, p. 7 (bottom); © dpa picture alliance/Alamy, p. 8; © Ronald Leunis/EyeEm/Getty Images, p. 9; © iStockphoto.com/chrisncami, p. 10; © Paul Bruins Photography/Flickr RF/Getty Images, p. 11 (left); © Robert Shantz/Alamy, p. 11 (right); © Laura Westlund/Independent Picture Service, p. 12; © kapyos/Bigstock.com, p. 13; © Federico Veronesi/ Gallo Images/Getty Images, p. 14; © Johnny Madsen/Alamy, p. 15 (left); © Eric Woods/Photodisc/Getty Images, p. 15 (right); © iStockphoto.com/CarolinaBirdman, p. 16; © iStockphoto.com/MikeLane45, p. 17 (top); © iStockphoto.com/Mirko_Rosenau, p. 17 (bottom); © Minden Pictures/SuperStock, p. 18; © Suzi Eszterhas/naturepl.com, p. 19; © NHPA/Photoshot , p. 20; © Bruce Coleman/Photoshot, p. 21; © Sarah Darnell/SuperStock, p. 22; © Angelika Stern/E+/Getty Images, p. 23 (left); © Nick Saunders/Flickr RF/Getty Images, p. 23 (right); © Doug Cheeseman/Photolibrary RM/Getty Images, p. 24; © Kat Sicard/Alamy, p. 25; (top); © iStockphoto.com/estivillml, p. 25 (bottom); © Juniors Bildarchiv/GmbH/Alamy, p. 26; © Denis-Huot/ naturepl.com, p. 27 (top); © Animals Animals/SuperStock, p. 27 (middle); © Arco Images/GmbH/Alamy, p. 27 (bottom); © All Canada Photos/Alamy, p. 28; © FLPA/Alamy, p. 29 (left); © Charles Melton/Visuals Unlimited, Inc., p. 29 (right).

Front cover: © Peter Chadwick/Gallo Images/Getty Images
Back cover: © Andrzej Kubik/Shutterstock.com

Main body text set in Calvert MT Std 12/18. Typeface provided by Monotype Typography.

Library of Congress Cataloging-in-Publication Data

Waxman, Laura Hamilton, author.
    Ostriches : fast flightless birds / Laura Hamilton Waxman.
        pages cm. — (Comparing animal traits)
    Summary: "This book covers information (life cycle, appearance, habitat) about the ostrich. Each chapter discusses an aspect of the ostrich's life, comparing the bird to a similar bird and to a very different bird."— Provided by publisher.
    Audience: Ages 7-10.
    Audience: K to grade 3.
    Includes bibliographical references and index.
    ISBN 978-1-4677-9509-8 (lb : alk. paper) — ISBN 978-1-4677-9633-0 (pb : alk. paper) — ISBN 978-1-4677-9634-7 (eb pdf)
    1. Ostriches—Juvenile literature. I. Title.
QL696.S9W39 2016
598.5'24—dc23   2015017441

Manufactured in the United States of America
1 – BP – 12/31/15

TABLE OF CONTENTS ... 4

MEET THE OSTRICH

An ostrich stretches its long neck and takes a good look around. With its large eyes, it spots a lion in the distance and quickly sprints away. Ostriches are a kind of bird. Other kinds of animals you may know are insects, reptiles, amphibians, fish, and mammals.

Ostriches run through the grass.

All birds share certain traits. Birds are vertebrates—animals with backbones. Birds have feathers and a beak. Birds are warm-blooded. Their body temperature stays the same, even when the temperature around them changes. Birds also lay hard-shelled eggs. Ostriches share these traits with other birds. But some traits make ostriches stand out.

CHAPTER 1

WHAT DO OSTRICHES LOOK LIKE?

Ostriches are the largest bird species in the world. They weigh up to 350 pounds (159 kilograms). They stand up to 9 feet (2.7 meters) tall. That's taller than any human. Their long, strong legs make ostriches excellent sprinters. They also have sturdy feet and sharp claws. Ostriches are the only bird with just two toes on each foot.

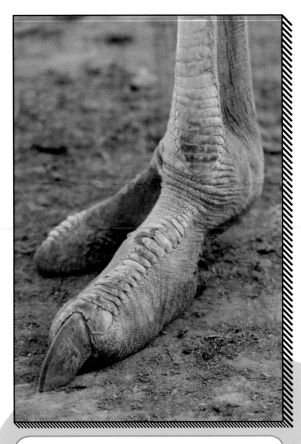

Ostriches do not fly. Their small wings cannot lift ostriches off the ground. Ostriches have drooping wing and tail feathers and fluffy body feathers. A male ostrich's feathers are mostly black. Its wing and tail feathers are white-tipped. Female ostriches have brown feathers that blend in with their habitat.

Do you see the claw on this ostrich's toe?

A pair of ostriches drink water.

Ostriches have a long neck and a small head. Their beak is flat and rounded at the tip. Their eyes are the largest of any land animal. They also have long eyelashes, a rare trait among birds. The eyelashes are made of small feathers. They protect an ostrich's eyes from blowing dirt and sand.

DID YOU KNOW?
An ostrich's scientific name is *Struthio camelus*, which means "camel bird." Both camels and ostriches have a **LONG NECK**, small head, and big eyelashes.

OSTRICHES VS. GREATER RHEAS

A greater rhea dashes across open grassland on fast-moving legs. Greater rheas are the largest birds in South America. They look a lot like ostriches.

Greater rheas have three toes on each foot.

Greater rheas are about 5 feet (1.5 m) tall. They weigh around 50 pounds (23 kg). Their round body is shaped like a large football, similar to an ostrich's body. Like ostriches, these birds have a long neck and small head. They also have eyelashes and a rounded beak.

Greater rheas have loose, fluffy feathers. The feathers are mostly grayish brown. Like ostriches, greater rheas do not fly. But they are fast runners. Both birds have long, strong legs and tough feet. When running, the birds use their large wings for balance.

Greater rheas, like ostriches, have powerful eyesight and hearing.

OSTRICHES VS. VERMILION FLYCATCHERS

A vermilion flycatcher darts through the air. It snatches an insect in its pointy beak. Vermilion flycatchers are tiny compared to ostriches. They are only about 5 inches (13 centimeters) long from beak to tail. They weigh about half an ounce (14 grams). That's about the same as three nickels. Vermilion flycatchers stand on short, skinny legs. Each foot has four toes for perching in trees.

Unlike ostriches, male vermilion flycatchers are brightly colored. Their head and chest are a bold red. Their dark-colored wings are suited for swift flight. Vermilion flycatchers have small eyes and no eyelashes. Their black beak is pointed at the tip.

A vermilion flycatcher perches on a branch.

COMPARE IT!

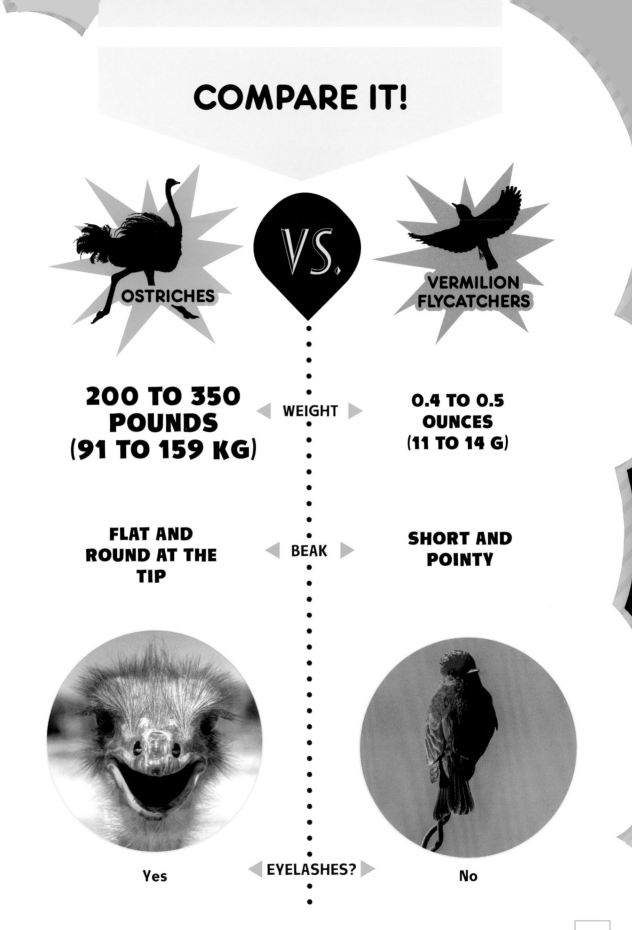

OSTRICHES **VS.** VERMILION FLYCATCHERS

200 TO 350 POUNDS (91 TO 159 KG)	◄ WEIGHT ►	**0.4 TO 0.5 OUNCES (11 TO 14 G)**
FLAT AND ROUND AT THE TIP	◄ BEAK ►	**SHORT AND POINTY**
Yes	◄ EYELASHES? ►	No

CHAPTER 2

WHERE DO OSTRICHES LIVE?

Ostriches are birds of Africa. They live in dry grasslands and other dry, open habitats with sand or sandy soil. They look for places with enough plants to eat. Ostriches often **graze** on plants near other grazing animals, such as zebras and giraffes.

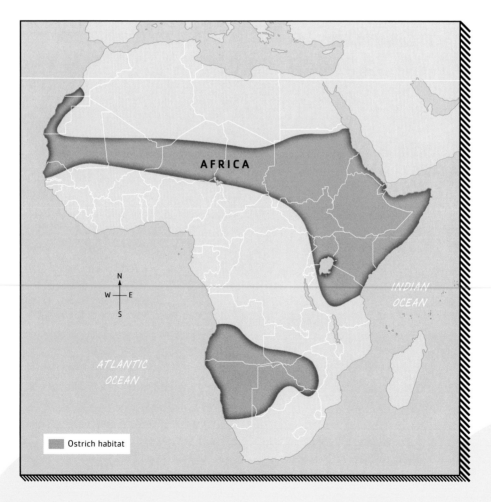

AFRICA

INDIAN OCEAN

N
W · E
S

ATLANTIC OCEAN

Ostrich habitat

The temperature in the ostrich's habitat can be a challenge. During the day, the blazing sun beats down. Ostriches move their wings away from their body to allow heat to escape more easily. At night, temperatures can be much colder. To stay warm, ostriches cover their bare upper legs with their fluffy wings.

Another challenge ostriches face is finding drinking water. They sometimes find water in their habitat. But they get most of their water from the food they eat.

DID YOU KNOW?
Ostriches once lived in southwestern Asia. They were wiped out due to **OVERHUNTING.** Ostriches were hunted for their feathers. The feathers were a popular decoration for women's hats and clothing.

OSTRICHES VS. SECRETARY BIRDS

A secretary bird flies down from its nest in the morning. On long legs, it begins to hunt for snakes and other animals in the tall grass. Secretary birds are African birds, like ostriches. They also live in a similar habitat.

Secretary birds seek open spaces, especially grasslands. Ostriches and secretary birds avoid hilly areas and places with trees that are close together.

A secretary bird's flat, open habitat makes it easier to find food. Secretary birds hunt for animals on the ground. They need space to find and chase down their prey. Ostriches seek open habitats to search for grass seed and other plants on the ground. A flat, open habitat also helps them keep an eye out for predators.

A secretary bird eats a snake it has hunted.

COMPARE IT!

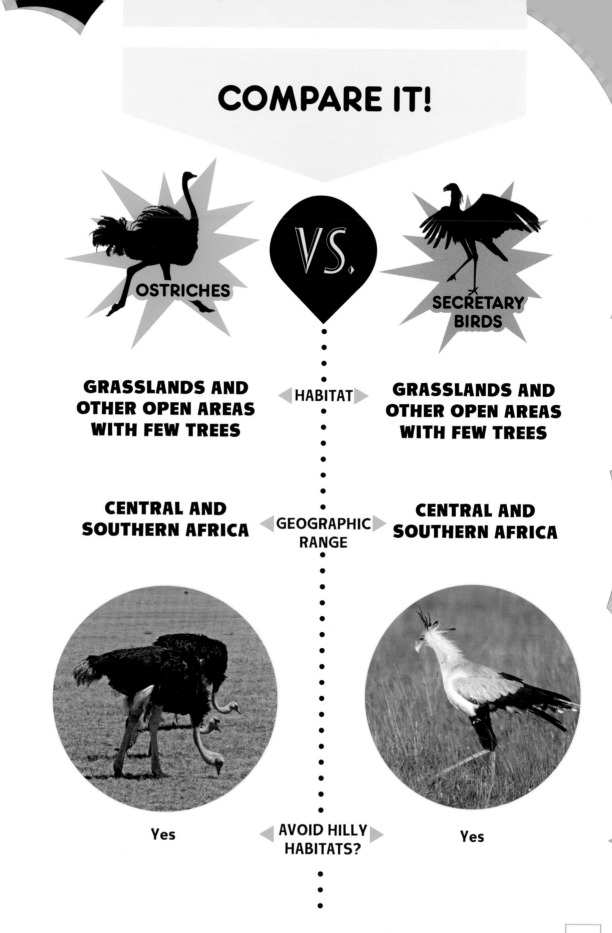

OSTRICHES

VS.

SECRETARY BIRDS

◄ HABITAT ►

GRASSLANDS AND OTHER OPEN AREAS WITH FEW TREES

GRASSLANDS AND OTHER OPEN AREAS WITH FEW TREES

◄ GEOGRAPHIC RANGE ►

CENTRAL AND SOUTHERN AFRICA

CENTRAL AND SOUTHERN AFRICA

◄ AVOID HILLY HABITATS? ►

Yes

Yes

OSTRICHES VS. TUNDRA SWANS

A tundra swan dips its head underwater. With its strong bill, it plucks a tasty plant. Tundra swans spend their entire lives near and in water. They seek shallow pools, lakes, and wide rivers. These wet habitats provide tundra swans with plenty of aquatic plants to eat. Tundra swans also eat shellfish that live in their habitat.

> Near the end of summer, tundra swans fly south to spend the winter in warmer places.

In late spring and summer, Tundra swans live in the wetlands of the Arctic tundra. At this time of year, the sun shines almost twenty-four hours a day. Even so, daytime temperatures stay cool. The average summer temperature is 37°F–54°F (3°C–12°C).

DID YOU KNOW?
Unlike ostriches, tundra swans live in many parts of the world. Their **WETLAND** habitats can be found in North America, Asia, Africa, Europe, and the islands of the Caribbean.

CHAPTER 3

OSTRICHES IN ACTION

An ostrich lowers its head to the dry grass at its feet. With its flat beak, it plucks some seeds. It swallows quickly, then plucks some more. The ostrich moves slowly as it grazes, plucking and swallowing again and again.

Ostriches are omnivores. They mostly eat plants. Less often, they eat insects and other small animals. Ostriches have no way to chew their food. They must swallow pebbles, which grind the food in their gizzard.

Two ostriches search the ground for food.

While grazing, ostriches often raise their head to look for predators. Lions, leopards, and hyenas are common ostrich predators. Ostriches can sprint from danger at more than 40 miles (64 kilometers) per hour. That makes these birds the fastest two-legged animals on Earth. Ostriches are also powerful fighters. They can kick a predator hard enough to kill it.

Ostriches fight each other too. A male ostrich will defend its territory. It hisses and flaps its wings to scare off other males. It shoves with its chest and kicks with its legs.

DID YOU KNOW?
There's an old belief that scared ostriches hide their head in the sand. This is not true. Ostriches sometimes hide from predators by lying **FLAT** on the ground with their neck outstretched. This makes it look as if their head is buried.

OSTRICHES VS. DWARF CASSOWARIES

A dwarf cassowary picks up a piece of fruit from the ground on the large island of New Guinea. Then it swallows the fruit whole. Dwarf cassowaries are flightless birds, like ostriches. They defend themselves from predators in similar ways too. Both birds are able to outrun their predators. A dwarf cassowary can run up to 30 miles (48 km) per hour. A kick from its strong legs can be deadly.

Dwarf cassowaries have strong legs and sharp claws.

Dwarf cassowaries are omnivores, the same as ostriches. They mostly eat fallen fruit or fruit from low shrubs. They also hunt insects, lizards, and small mammals.

Like ostriches, dwarf cassowaries do not chew their food. They swallow it whole. Fruit seeds remain whole when they leave the birds' bodies in droppings. Dwarf cassowaries play an important role by spreading these fruit seeds throughout their rain forest home.

Dwarf cassowaries have a hard ridge on their head. The ridge protects the birds from thorny plants as they run through the forest.

OSTRICHES VS. MERLINS

A merlin zooms through the air, catching a smaller bird in mid-flight. Merlins are carnivores. They are known for their surprise, high-speed attacks. Merlins hunt mostly small birds but will also eat insects and other animals.

Merlins often perch in trees as they search for an animal to eat. When they spot prey on the ground, merlins attack it from above. If the prey is a flying bird, they may zoom down and surprise it from below. Merlins chase another bird until it is too worn out to escape. Once merlins have caught their prey, they return to their perch to eat. They tear apart food with their sharp, hooked beak. Unlike ostriches, adult merlins don't have many predators.

A merlin watches for prey.

COMPARE IT!

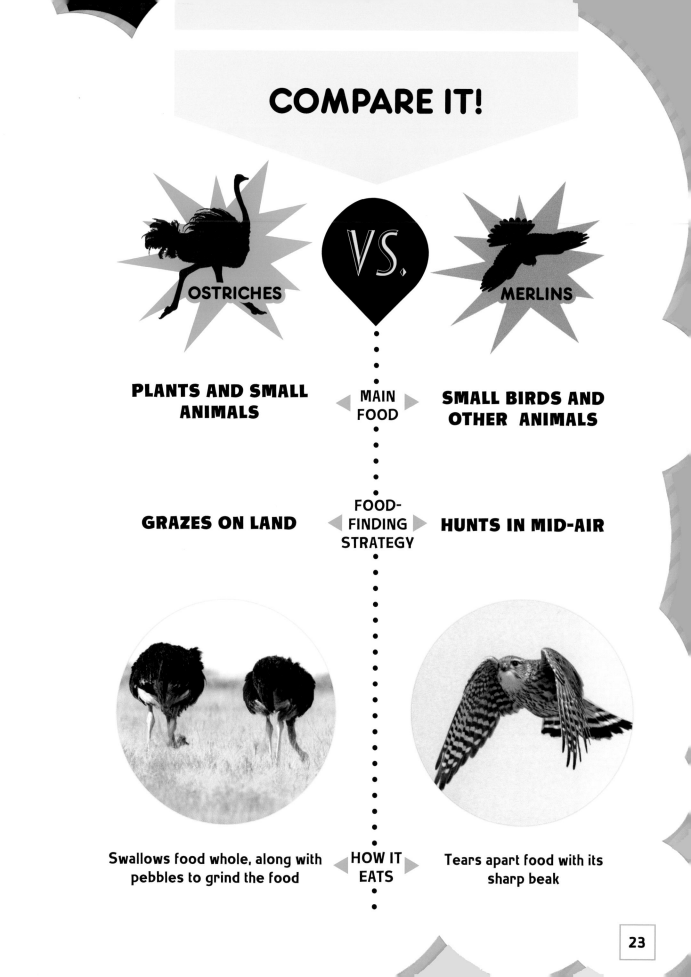

OSTRICHES

VS.

MERLINS

PLANTS AND SMALL ANIMALS ◄ MAIN FOOD ► **SMALL BIRDS AND OTHER ANIMALS**

GRAZES ON LAND ◄ FOOD-FINDING STRATEGY ► **HUNTS IN MID-AIR**

Swallows food whole, along with pebbles to grind the food ◄ HOW IT EATS ► Tears apart food with its sharp beak

CHAPTER 4

THE LIFE CYCLE OF OSTRICHES

Ostriches live in small groups that usually have one male and three to five females. The male uses his feet to dig a wide nest on the ground. The dominant female lays her eggs first. She is the strongest female in the group. The other females, called hens, lay their eggs in the same nest. Each hen lays up to ten eggs. Only the dominant female and the male incubate the eggs. The male sits on the nest at night, when his dark feathers make him hard for predators to see. The female sits on the nest during the day. Her lighter-colored feathers blend in with the ground around her.

The heat from a female ostrich's body helps keep her eggs warm.

DID YOU KNOW?
Ostrich eggs are the **HEAVIEST** eggs of any living bird. They usually weigh more than 3 pounds (1.4 kg).

After about six weeks, the eggs hatch. Ostrich chicks are born with soft, spiky feathers. They leave the nest with their parents after a few days. The male and dominant female raise all the chicks.

A male ostrich with chicks

Ostriches get many traits from their parents. A month after hatching, ostrich chicks can run nearly 35 miles (56 km) per hour. They grow quickly too. In six months, they're almost as tall as their parents. Ostriches are fully mature and ready to mate when they are three to four years old. Ostriches may live up to forty years.

OSTRICHES VS. COMMON PHEASANTS

Korrk-kok! A male common pheasant calls out to a female pheasant. He flaps his wings to get her attention. Common pheasants share a similar life cycle with ostriches. Like ostriches, one male common pheasant mates with a group of females. There may be as many as eighteen females in one group.

Like ostriches, common pheasants make nests on the ground. The nests are bowl-shaped and made of grass. Each female lays six to fifteen eggs. They hatch about twenty-four days later. The male pheasant raises the chicks with the females.

Common pheasant eggs are much smaller than ostrich eggs.

Like ostriches, common pheasant chicks are covered in soft feathers. They can walk right away, and they follow their parents to find food. Common pheasants are fully grown and ready to mate after one year. They live for about three years.

An ostrich chick (*top*) and a common pheasant chick (*bottom*) just after hatching

DID YOU KNOW?

Common pheasants are also called ring-necked pheasants for the bright white ring of feathers around their neck.

OSTRICHES VS. MOURNING DOVES

A mourning dove busily pecks at the ground. It picks up seeds and crunches them in its beak. Mourning doves have a different life cycle than ostriches. Unlike ostriches, mourning doves seek a single mate. The male and female carefully build a nest in a tree with sticks, pine needles, and grass.

The female lays two eggs that hatch after two weeks. Her chicks are born without feathers. They are helpless and depend completely on their parents. The parents regurgitate food into the chicks' mouths.

The chicks are strong enough to leave the nest after about fifteen days. They are fully grown after only twelve weeks. Mourning doves live for about eighteen months.

A pair of mourning doves

COMPARE IT!

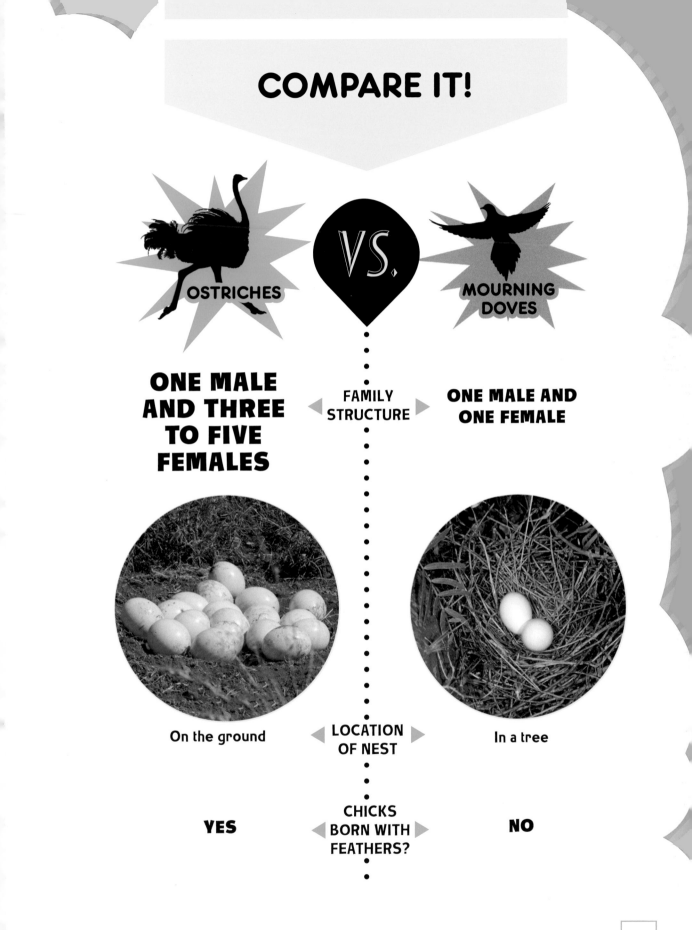

OSTRICHES

VS.

MOURNING DOVES

ONE MALE AND THREE TO FIVE FEMALES

◀ FAMILY STRUCTURE ▶

ONE MALE AND ONE FEMALE

On the ground

◀ LOCATION OF NEST ▶

In a tree

YES

◀ CHICKS BORN WITH FEATHERS? ▶

NO

OSTRICH TRAIT CHART

This book introduces ostriches and compares them to other birds. What other birds would you like to compare?

	WARM-BLOODED	FEATHERS ON BODY	LAYS HARD-SHELLED EGGS	FLIGHTLESS BIRD	EYELASHES	OMNIVORE
OSTRICH	X	X	X	X	X	X
GREATER RHEA	X	X	X	X	X	X
VERMILION FLYCATCHER	X	X	X			
SECRETARY BIRD	X	X	X		X	
TUNDRA SWAN	X	X	X			X
DWARF CASSOWARY	X	X	X	X	X	X
MERLIN	X	X	X			
COMMON PHEASANT	X	X	X			X
MOURNING DOVE	X	X	X			X

aquatic: found in or near water

Arctic tundra: a northern region where the ground is always frozen and there are no trees

beak: the jaws and mouth of a bird. Beaks are also called bills, especially when they are long and flat.

carnivores: meat-eating animals

dominant: more important or powerful than other members of a group

gizzard: a part in a bird's stomach where food is crushed

graze: to feed on plants throughout the day

habitat: an environment where an animal naturally lives

incubate: to keep eggs warm and under good conditions before they hatch

omnivores: animals that eat both plants and meat

predators: animals that hunt, or prey on, other animals

prey: an animal that is hunted and killed by a predator for food

regurgitate: to bring swallowed food back up into the mouth

species: animals that share common features and can produce offspring

territory: an area that is occupied and defended by an animal or a group of animals

traits: features that are inherited from parents, such as body size and feather color

SELECTED BIBLIOGRAPHY

Donegan, Keenan. "*Struthio camelus*: Ostrich." *Animal Diversity Web*. Accessed August 6, 2015. http://animaldiversity. org/accounts/Struthio_camelus/.

Harrison, Colin, and Alan Greensmith. *Birds of the World*. New York: DK, 1993.

Murchie, Jason. "*Struthio camelus*, the Common Ostrich." *Tree of Life*. Accessed August 6, 2015. http://tolweb.org/ treehouses/?treehouse_id=4734.

Sibley, David. *The Sibley Guide to Bird Life & Behavior*. New York: Alfred A. Knopf, 2001.

FURTHER INFORMATION

Johnson, Jinny. *Animal Planet™ Atlas of Animals*. Minneapolis: Millbrook Press, 2012. Travel around the world and explore the planet's incredible animal diversity in this richly illustrated book.

National Geographic: Ostrich
http://animals.nationalgeographic.com/ animals/birds/ostrich
Visit this *National Geographic* website for ostrich facts and photos.

San Diego Zoo: Ostrich
http://animals.sandiegozoo.org/animals/ ostrich
Discover all kinds of unusual facts about ostriches at the San Diego Zoo's website.

Wildscreen Arkive: Ostrich
http://www.arkive.org/ostrich/struthio- camelus
Learn more about ostriches with this website's photos and facts.

INDEX